AFFIRMATIONS LITE
THE ESSENTIALS

WELCOME to the WONDERFUL WORLD OF AFFIRMATIONS
WHERE DREAMS CAN AND DO COME TRUE!

Dr. Anne Marie Evers

Discover and Learn how to write effective, powerful, and results-oriented affirmations to make your fondest dreams come true using the method outlined in this book.

Copyright © 2017
Published in Canada by Affirmations International Publishing
Company.
All rights reserved, including the right to reproduce this book or any
portion thereof in any form.

Queries regarding rights and permissions:
Dr. Anne Marie Evers,
Affirmations International Publishing Company,
4559 Underwood Avenue,
North Vancouver, BC, Canada,
V7K 2S3
Fax 1-604-904-1127
Email: annemarieevers@shaw.ca
www.heretohelpsolutions.com
ISBN# 978-1-926995-10-6

Also by the author:
Affirmations Your Passport to Happiness 8th edition

Disclaimer

The information provided in this book/e-book is for educational
purposes only and is not intended to be used, nor should it be used, to
treat any medical or psychological condition. For diagnosis or treatment,
always consult your physician or other health care professionals. You are
advised to talk to your doctor and/or healthcare professional about your
specific medical condition and/or treatments and the use of these
strategies outlined in this book.
The information in this book may be helpful and may act as a supportive
and complimentary tool to the recommended treatment by a health care
professional, but it is not a substitute for professional diagnosis or
treatment.

TABLE OF CONTENTS

IMPORTANT NOTE

Many people think that affirmations should happen immediately or in their predetermined time frame and as they expect them to manifest. Be open to expect the unexpected or something better. Writing and saying your affirmations are the first steps to creating and/or recreating your life and to make your dreams come true.
This will become clearer as you read this book.

FOREWORD

"There are two ways of creating your reality—by consciously programming what we want out of life or by simply accepting what comes our way. Both work, but only the former will ensure that you get what you want in life. Doing the Affirmation Program helps put you in charge of your programming and consequently firmly in control of your life. As you use affirmations daily and consistently, you will be breathing life into the future of your dreams.

Dr. Lee Pulos, Ph. D.,
Foreword to Affirmations Your Passport to Happiness
6th, 7th and 8th editions

OUR RESEARCH SHOWS THE TOP SEVEN REASONS FOR PEOPLE DOING AFFIRMATIONS

-1-
RELATIONSHIPS

-2-
CAREER

-3-
MONEY

-4-
HEALTH

-5-
FORGIVENESS

-6-
SELF-ESTEEM

-7-
GREATER SPIRITUAL AWARENESS

CHAPTER 1 THE W

of Affirmations

What

An affirmation is like a birthday wish or a goal that is more structured and specific. *The basis of all affirmations is positive thinking.*

Who

Everyone and anyone from children to adults.

Where

Any place, at work, in the privacy of your own home, at school, while exercising, walking, or waiting in line at a store, for a friend or at a doctor/dentist's office.

WE ALL DO AFFIRMATIONS!

 **hen**

Whenever you wish to do them. We recommend saying your affirmations at least twice daily or more for a 21 day period. It is best to do them the first thing in the morning and the last thing in the evening before going to bed.

 **hy**

Affirmations are done to change a behaviour, create a new habit, eliminate an old habit, and give you the opportunity to recreate your life.

Consider This

"If you were powerful enough to create your present life
by the choices you made,
you can recreate it
by making new and different choices
using the same energy and commitment."

You will discover the **HOW** of Affirmations later in this book.

CHAPTER 2

The 5 Building Blocks

THE AFFIRMATION CONTRACT PROCESS

5 — Creative Visualizations

4 — Affirmations

3 — Mind Power

2 — Power of Thoughts

1 — Forgiveness & Release

When you write your Affirmation using the 5 Building Blocks, you have a solid and firm foundation upon which to write a <u>successful</u> Affirmation.

Dr. Anne Marie Evers, D.D

Forgiveness and Releasing

Forgiveness

- o is the very first and most important Building Block

- o is very powerful

- o is a choice

Forgiveness promotes:
- o good health, friendships, happy families, reduces stress, lowers blood pressure, increases, well-being

<u>Consider This</u>
Forgiveness is private.

When you do not forgive another person, you remain focused on them and the problem.

When you forgive yourself and others, you benefit the most.

Real, true forgiveness heals even the deepest of wounds.

The Toothbrush Forgiveness Affirmation
Do this affirmation while brushing your teeth.

"I, (your name) now forgive everyone and everything that has *ever* hurt me. I now forgive myself and am forgiven. I love, respect and approve of myself just the way I am."

the wedding and

the toothbrush

The Wedding and the Toothbrush

This is a story about a woman and her soon-to-be husband. She wanted him to do the Extended Toothbrush Affirmation Life Tool Activity as it worked so well for her. He reluctantly agreed to do it and he told her that things started to percolate in his mind regarding persons and situations.

He also said that he needed to forgive people and one of them was his dad. Up to this point he was not speaking to his dad and while doing the Extended Toothbrush Affirmation Life Tool, he was able to forgive his dad and happily invited him to his wedding.

Tommy's Story from the Third Grade

Tommy, a third grader, learned about the Extended Toothbrush Exercise. After class he said to me, "You know Dr. Evers, I cannot do that Toothbrush Exercise...cause I don't love myself." I asked him to do it the best he could. He agreed and we shook hands.

Three weeks later I returned to the school and Tommy came running up to me. He said, excitedly, "I did it! I did it! You know what you told me to do...You know that tooth brush thing and now I love myself! And I like and respect others too."

Power of Thoughts

Thoughts are very powerful!
Thoughts become things.
As one thinks, so one becomes.
Thoughts attract people/situations that resonate with the originating thought.
When thoughts are held in mind, they form a life of their own and attract others of similar thought.

A thought
- is a force as real as a current of electricity
- always attempts to find a pathway through which to express itself and create what you want

Consider This
You, and you alone, are in control of your thoughts.
You cannot jump into another person's mind and think their thoughts for them, nor can anyone jump into your mind and think your thoughts for you!
To be successful, you need to harness and focus on the great and wonderful power of the mind.
You must learn to 'Deliberately Control' and "Direct" the powerful thought processes of the mind by placing a gatekeeper at the entrance of your mind!

The Cat that Wasn't There!

When I was a real estate agent, I had a client who was allergic to animals, especially cats. She instructed me to ONLY show her homes and apartments that did not have cats. On one of my showings, while I was checking on something in the kitchen, she went into one of the bedrooms and came running out screaming, "There's a cat in there. I told you -- **NO CATS**! I am allergic to cats". She went into the living room, dropped on the sofa with her eyes watering and gasping for air. I went into the bedroom, picked up the *stuffed cat* off the bed and showed her. She looked at me not believing it was a *stuffed cat* that she saw. She went into the bedroom to make sure that there was not another live cat and that I was telling the truth. After having proved to herself that there was not a live cat in the apartment, all the symptoms left . She felt rather foolish about the whole situation.

P.S. No, she did **NOT** buy the property!

I was amazed that her mind triggered the physical results it did. In her mind she saw a cat and experienced it as real which resulted in her much anticipated negative reaction to cats. Imagine the power of your thoughts!

Mind Power

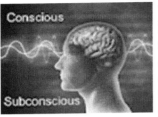

The mind has two distinct, yet interrelated functions.
Conscious mind is the conscious, objective, outward or waking state (of what you are aware, such as thoughts, ideas, concepts, etc.).
Subconscious mind is the subjective, inward or sleeping state. (Inner-programing--automatic and hidden).

I liken the conscious mind to the captain of a ship who gives the orders to the crew (the subconscious mind) who obey the captain's orders immediately and without question.
Your subconscious mind is your humble servant always willing and anxious to please you and carry out your orders via your conscious mind. How are you instructing *your* subconscious mind?

The following story, about my cousin Alice, has always reminded me of the power of the mind.

Alice and the Cheese Cake

alice and the cheese cake

Did someone say cheese?

When I was a child, it became quite clear to me how thoughts and the power of the mind affect our lives. At a dinner party one evening, my Aunt Bea served a delicious cream dessert. Everyone raved about it and most of the guests requested a second helping. Four hours later, someone asked Aunt Bea for the recipe. She started to name the ingredients and, when she came to cream cheese, my cousin Alice gasped, put her hand over her mouth, ran to the bathroom, and vomited.

It turned out that Alice was extremely allergic to cream cheese! I could not understand her reaction and asked my mother why it took Alice so long to get sick. Nor could I understand why she became so violently ill when she heard those two harmless words, *cream cheese*. My mother said, "It has something to do with thoughts and her mind, dear. Don't worry, she will be okay."

Affirmations

<u>Affirmations</u> - Your Order to the Universe. Call up and place your order NOW! Operators are standing by to take your call. All calls are local calls! NO Long Distance charges applied!

Affirmations are more effective when written as you anchor the words to your subconscious mind where they reside. A properly written affirmation becomes a new contributing blueprint of your life.

Affirmations are specific statements. Make your affirmations as clear and concise as possible.

Affirmations can be re-written as you change and/or as you become clearer about what it is that you want.

Consider This
Whenever you are goal setting with powerful, focused intent, you are doing a form of an affirmation.

So, take time and enjoy the journey and your results!

Today, I have the perfect part time career in a professional office where my fellow workers have a great sense of humor!

Perfect, Lasting, Successful Career

A lady in our class was doing an affirmation for the perfect, lasting, successful career. She complained that her affirmation was not working. When asked what she wanted, she said she wanted *a part-time* position.

The affirmation was re-written to include this clarification for a part time position. Within a week her affirmation came true and even surpassed her expectations. She now works in an office that is filled with humour and harmony.

THEREFORE...

Choose your WORDS wisely.
Words have meaning!
Words contain a
POSITIVE or NEGATIVE
electrical and emotional charge
that is only known to you.

In other words,
WORDS trigger an EMOTIONAL RESPONSE
that is
SPECIFIC to YOU
and your lived experience!

Creative Visualization

Thinking, Feeling and Talking in Pictures

Creative Visualization is a structured and directed practice. Scientific studies have shown that the images and activities that you create in your mind are just as real as if the event is actually taking place.

When you practice creative visualization and imaging, you are transporting yourself into a future situation and lived-experience that has not yet taken place.

Since your mind does not know the difference between a real event and an imagined event, it accepts your visualization as truth, as fact.

To enrich the Affirmation Process, artists, coaches, professional athletes and other successful business people use creative visualization in their daily lives with exceptional success.

5 SENSES and Neuro-Linguistic Programming (NLP)

People process information differently. NLP has taught us that some individuals are visual (sight), others are auditory (hearing), some are kinesthetic (touch/feel), a few are gustatory (taste), and very few are olfactory (smell).

An additional category has been added to NLP in recent years which is identified as Auditory-Digital (AD). The focus of AD is on the exact meaning of words being expressed by the individual. The exact words used and their meaning is central to communication, which is revealed in the individual's active inner self-talk life and external expressive verbiage in which the person engages.

caroline and the machine

Teeing off with radiation therapy

Caroline and the Machine

The most important affirmation I did was asking for healing during a prolonged medical treatment. I affirmed over and over, "I am becoming healthier and healthier."

To keep from being afraid, I visualized myself playing golf at my favourite golf course. It worked! I got my mind focusing on and thinking about something positive and happy. As a result, I regained my health.

Having Difficulty with Creative Visualization ? Try This ...

1. Create a collage that expresses what you want to have come into your life.
2. Place various scents/fragrances on it.
3. While looking at your collage (virtual affirmation), drink a favorite beverage or eat a favorite food; also listen to and/or hum/sing your favorite tune.
4. Commit the experience to memory through repetition.

NLP YOUR AFFIRMATIONS

Enrich your affirmations with the dominant way you communicate with yourself and others.

1. **Visual** (I see! Looks good to me! I can see it now!)

Add pictures graphic images, lots of colour to your affirmations; paint it; draw it; frame it! Use it as a wallpaper on your computer or smart devices. See your affirmation coming to pass.

2. Auditory (I hear what you are saying! Sounds good to me!)

Add sound, music, and rhyming to your affirmation. Write it as a poem to yourself. Sing, record it, and place it on your computer or smart devices to listen to often throughout the day. Hear your affirmation coming to pass.

3. Kinesthetic (Feels good to me! That's rough! The presentation was like listening to sandpaper)

Create a physical, three dimensional representation of your affirmation. Include lots of objects that reflect your favourite items to touch, such as cotton, silk, the touch of the grain of wood, bark, etc. Write your affirmation on a piece of tree bark, white birch, or a silk handkerchief that you can take with you. Feel your affirmation coming to pass.

4. Gustatory (Sweet!) or **5. Olfactory** (The smell of success)

Bring your favourite scent or food (fruit) with you. When you say your affirmation, spray the scent and/or eat the fruit, vegetable, favourite food stuff. Taste or smell your affirmation coming to pass.

6. Auditory-Digital (specific and concise words used to describe situations in one's inner self-talk and expressed life.)

Create your affirmation with the exact words that best describe what you want. Create a word collage or word board. Put it on your digital devices and take it with you. Describe your affirmation coming to pass with precision.

CHAPTER 3

THE Affirmation Garden

FOUR STEPS TO DOING AN AFFIRMATION

STEP 1 – Soil Preparation
Prepare the rich, fertile soil of your subconscious mind to receive the tender seed, (*Master Affirmation*) by releasing and forgiving everyone and everything that has ***ever*** hurt you. *When doing your forgiveness, should too many negative memories surface at the same time, simply say with authority, "One at a time please." Then deal with that one completely before going on to the next one.*

STEP 2 – Seed Selection
Create your Master Affirmation. Be very specific. Say exactly what you desire. Add an element of excitement by appealing to your five physical senses which will awaken and excite the subconscious mind!

STEP 3 – Water and Fertilize Your Seed (*Master Affirmation*)
Care for your Affirmation by reading it in the morning and evening on a daily basis. Make it mobile by bringing it with you in paper or electronic format.

 STEP 4 -- Anticipate the Harvest
Step ahead 2-3 weeks or months, feel and experience your affirmation as affirmed. Act as though it has already take place.

Consider This

People plant seeds with the expectation that they are going to grow. In other words, they believe that the plants will grow.

APPLY this **Principle of Growth** to your affirmation writing and outcome!

The Believe-ability Factor and Who is in Charge?

The Situation
I have 49%.
The other (person or company) has 51%.
(The other has the controlling interest.)

The Situation
I have 50%.
The other has 50%.
(Stalemate unless both agree.)

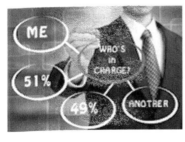

The Situation
I have 51%.
The other has 49%.
(I have controlling interest.)

Consider This

You need to have at least a 51% believe-ability factor for your affirmations to succeed.

CHAPTER 4 Writing Affirmations

HOW TO WRITE A SUCCESSFUL AFFIRMATION

"Your books are like recipe books, providing a step-by-step approach to making things happen. Great Stuff!" J.W.

Definitions
Master Affirmation – Your Order to the Universe
The Master Affirmation or Long Form Affirmation is the complete written affirmations expressing exactly what it is you desire. Make it as specific, clear, concise, and detailed as possible.

Short Form Affirmation (SFA)
The Short Form Affirmation highlights several key words taken from the Master Affirmation, which can be jotted down or repeated several times during the day.

<u>Consider This</u>
Doing both the Master Affirmation and Short Form Affirmation daily keeps your affirmation on the front burner of your mind and speeds up the manifestation of what you want to create.

Ways of Repeating Your Daily Affirmations – written, record,
spoken, silent-saying it to yourself, wallpaper, screen-saver, ipod, smart phone recording, and use of other technology.

Affirmation Hint

Before starting to create your Master Affirmation, take time to decide what you really want. Is your affirmation for something you want or what someone else wants for you?

Once you decide exactly what you desire, then start composing your Master Affirmation.

Master Affirmation

When doing an affirmation, use the following format.

SAMPLE MASTER AFFIRMATION CONTRACT

(Place picture, photo or sketch of what you desire here)

I, (your name) *deserve* and now have/am

_____

_____

_____

_____

to the good of all parties concerned. Thank you, thank you, thank you.

I fully accept

Signed:_____ Dated:_____

Note: The Master Affirmation is created only **ONCE** and then it can be changed, added to, subtracted from or re-written as you change and become clearer or you realize that you want something different, but only realized this as you wrote your affirmation.

Place your completed, dated and signed Master Affirmation into a plastic insert sheet for safe keeping.
Place each Master Affirmation on a separate page and store in an Affirmations Binder or scrapbook. Decorate and embellish as desired.

Additional Notes

1. Placing a picture or sketch of what you desire at the top of the page gives your subconscious mind something upon which to focus when affirming.

2. When you date and sign your Master Affirmation, you have made a firm and binding contract with God/Creator, Universal Mind, Your Higher Self or in whomever you believe.

3. You may choose to have one or more people to witness your Master Affirmation as this will ensure greater accountability.

4. Contracts/Agreements are worthless unless they are dated and signed by an authorized agent.

5. OPTION: Create a Mastermind Affirmation Group to be more accountable for your affirmations.
See Q.10 in Chapter 7 regarding the steps to setting up a Mastermind Group.

 **MASTER AFFIRMATION CONTRACT RULES**

Did you release any negative feelings, outdated beliefs or thoughts before doing your Affirmations?

Did you add the words, "I, (your name) _deserve and now have/am?_"

Do you feel that you deserve what you are affirming?

Is it worded to never hurt or take from anyone?

Did you include the safety clause, _"to the good of all parties concerned"_?

Is it specific, saying exactly what you desire?

Did you include the 3 P's - Personal, Positive, and Present Tense? _If you say, "will have"_, you are putting it off into the future, so always use the word 'now'.

Is there at least a 51% believe-ability factor that your affirmation can manifest as affirmed?

Is it colourful, exciting, and interesting? _Colour wakes up and excites the subconscious mind._

Did you say, "Thank you" three times?

Is your Acceptance Statement signed and dated?

Did you say, "Yes", to indicate you are ready to receive?

Did you check your rigid attachment to the outcome?

Is it heart-felt and emotionally-charged? Does it resonate with you?

Did you have fun?

If you answered *"Yes"* to all these questions, Congratulations, you have just completed your first Master Affirmation!

SHORT FORM AFFIRMATION
This consists of several key words taken from your Master Affirmation. Revisit it several times daily keeping it <u>on the front burner of your mind.</u>

SAMPLE SHORT FORM CAREER AFFIRMATION
Should you be affirming for that perfect, lasting, successful career for you where you are happy and fulfilled – your Short Form Affirmation would be:
Perfect, Happy Lasting Career – me now!

It is very important to say 'Me now' as you need to make it yours and ensure your right to and ownership of the affirmation!

Daily Practice

It is very important to deal completely with each Master Affirmation before going on to the next one to keep your mind focused and to avoid confusion. If you give a confused order, you may receive a confused answer or no answer at all.

The Process

Revisit your completed Master Affirmation at least every morning and evening to keep it refreshed in your mind. Read it. Commit it to memory. Repeat it several times a day, allowing each empowered word to sink deep into your subconscious mind where it takes root, grows and becomes your new reality.

Use your imagination and all your five senses. Step ahead several days, weeks, or months into your future. Experience the completion of your affirmation.

Consider This

When you have completed the above process for the Master Affirmation, go on about your day fully expecting and accepting the manifestation as affirmed or expect and accept something better.

JOB/CAREER MASTER AFFIRMATION

I, *(your name)* **deserve and now have** the perfect, lasting, successful career for me. I receive in excess of $ _____ (net or gross). My employers are very pleased with my excellent work and they reward me accordingly. I am happy, harmonious and fulfilled to the good of all parties concerned. Thank you, thank you, thank you.

I fully accept

Signed _____   Dated _____

SHORT FORM AFFIRMATION

Perfect, lasting, successful Career to me now!

Testimonial

Since reading your book and doing affirmations, I have increased my business and I am much more successful. Your book is in my office and lend it to clients and friends to read. May God keep blessing you as you bless others, Thank you, thank you, thank you. *G.W. Karate School*, New York, U.S.

* * *

Aren uses the affirmation process to meet monthly business targets. Because of her success, others are curious about her monthly successes. After she explains the process to them, they start to use it with success.

HEALTH MASTER AFFIRMATION

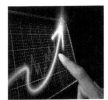

I, *(your name)* **deserve and now am** becoming healthier and healthier. Every cell, organ, muscle and every part of my body is now being filled with radiant health. I am thankful, healthy and happy to the good of all parties concerned. Thank you, thank you, thank you.

I fully accept

Signed _____ Dated _____

SHORT FORM AFFIRMATION

Healthier and Healthier - me now!

Healthier and healthier ...me now!

Testimonial

I think positive, uplifting affirmations are very helpful to everyone, but especially for those living with cancer or other health challenges, those undergoing chemotherapy and those in the last phase of life. A positive, uplifting approach helps to make the days meaningful and peaceful, while also providing a means of coming to terms with the realities of life. *Dr. Paul Sugar, Palliative Care Doctor*

* * *

I can usually tell by a patient's mental attitude if he/she will complete their chemo treatments. I was amazed at how Anne Marie's affirmation teachings transformed the lives of my patients. *Dr. Sasha Smilijanic, Chemotherapy Doctor*

MONEY/ PROSPERITY MASTER AFFIRMATION

I, *(your name)* **deserve and now receive** great wealth. Money flows to me in avenues of abundance which I use wisely. I also share my wonderful wealth with others to the good of all parties concerned. Thank you, thank you, thank you.

I fully accept

Signed _____Dated _____

SHORT FORM AFFIRM

Powerful money magnet – me now.

Powerful Money magnet ...me now!

MORE $UCCE$$

I worked fervently on the Prosperity Affirmations a couple of years ago and about 8 months later I won $50,000 on the California Lottery. I am once again doing affirmations for other things because I, for one, **KNOW THEY WORK!**

Eddie Corin, Los Angeles.

* * *

In the last 3 weeks since I have been doing the Money Affirmations that you teach, my practice has doubled! You really have touched on a Prosperity Formula here!

Tammy, Toronto, Canada

RELATIONSHIP MASTER AFFIRMATION

I, (your name) deserve and now have a loving, lasting, romantic, healthy, happy relationship with the perfect person for me. We share mutual interests and love and respect each other. We live together happily and harmoniously to the good of all parties concerned. Thank you, thank you, thank you.

I fully accept

Signed _____ *Dated* _____

SHORT FORM AFFIRMATION -

Lasting, Loving, Healthy Relationship - me now!

Affirmations Help Rebuild Our Marriage

We are working on re-building our marriage bringing back the love we had at the beginning. And we are doing well with the help of your Affirmation Program....

Ben, Manager, Hamilton, Ontario.

* * *

I just wanted to let you know that I did affirmations as set out in your book and it worked! I met the man of my dreams and we are engaged. I could not be happier. So many thanks to you. *Sue Anne Calgary, Alberta*

SELF-ESTEEM MASTER AFFIRMATION

I release all negative thoughts of past *so-called* failures and all thoughts of being unloved or unlovable. I love, respect, accept and approve of myself just the way I am to the good of all parties concerned. Thank you, thank you, thank you.

I fully accept

Signed _____ Dated _____

SHORT FORM - Loving and respecting -me now!

Testimonial

After practicing Affirmations, Ralph writes,

"Amazing, I know, but since I have increased my self-esteem, I received a huge promotion. I feel different about myself and others treat me so much better. Cheers!"

Ralph, Internet Programmer

THERE IS NOTHING LIKE AN ACCOMPLISHMENT TO PUT MORE STEAM IN YOUR SELF-ESTEEM!

SPIRITUAL GROWTH MASTER AFFIRMATION

I, (your name) deserve and now am open to receiving God's Love and Wisdom. Today I am filled with love, joy, peace, kindness, patience and contentment to the good of all parties concerned. Thank you, thank you, thank you.

I fully accept

Signed _____   Dated _____

SHORT FORM AFFIRMATION

Divine Wisdom & Divine Order – me now.

Testimonials

When I read your books and learned about affirmations and practiced them myself, I felt closer to God than I ever did. Thank you.

Leslie, student U.S.A.

* * *

Whether you know a lot about affirmations or are a newcomer to this field....Dr. Evers ... speaks from experience and testimonials. This is important because if you are a newcomer like me, reading how others have developed the capacity is important. In addition, she is not afraid to bring God into her teachings. *John De P. South America*

CHAPTER 5

Practicing Affirmations

DOING
EFFECTIVE
AFFIRMATION

BREATHE BREATH INTO YOUR AFFIRMATIONS BY TAKING ACTION

You can stand in an elevator all day long and affirm that it goes to the desired floor, but until you or someone else pushes the button to that floor, nothing happens. When doing affirmations, be sure to take the appropriate action. This is a very important part of the Affirmation Process.

MODUS OPERANDI

Never worry or concern yourself about the '*modus operandi*' (the way it happens).
You know the *What* you desire and God/Creator, Universal Mind, Higher Power or in whomever you believe knows the *How*. <u>Get</u> <u>out</u> <u>of</u> <u>the</u> <u>way</u> and trust the Law of Mind and Creation to take care of the rest.

REPETITION

We all know repetition is the Mother of Learning. When you repeat affirmations, thought patterns are impressed upon your subconscious mind. You replace your previously held beliefs, opinions, ideas and/or concepts with newer thought forms and neural pathways.

When you say affirmations over and over, the words become a living presence in your conscious awareness. Repetition re-enforces the belief system and convinces the mind that what is being affirmed is true.

The process of doing affirmations is not a one-time procedure or event. It requires constant repetition. Repetition of positive phrases increases the likelihood of the affirmation coming into existence and eliminating any negative subconscious programming.

RIGID ATTACHMENT TO OUTCOME

If you are too attached to what you want, you may miss what is already being manifested as the result of your affirmation. If you are too attached, you may miss attracting something better that has come or is coming into existence.

TIMING

Affirmations can—and sometimes do—manifest immediately, as if by magic. At other times, they take longer, requiring patience. Don't be discouraged if you don't see immediate results; simply imagine your manifestation being just around the corner.

WORDS

The words we speak and use in our affirmations are very powerful. Words are creative. We create with every word we speak! Words are powerful tools. They have a history and association all of their own, intertwined with our lived experience. Do some *thought/word watching*. You may be surprised at how many negative thoughts and words you entertain at any given time. Words can uplift, help raise you up or they can drag you down into the pit of despair.

Learn a Lesson from Nature

The lowly seed puts its roots and tiny tendrils down into the rich, fertile soil of the earth. It takes root and grows. At the same time, it sends sprouts up toward the light. When it encounters any obstacles, as it undoubtedly does, it is not discouraged. Instead, it simply goes around the obstacle, always stretching toward the life force of the sun and the air.

The little seed shows no lack of faith, nor does it question the length of time it will take to manifest as a flower, plant or tree. It simply acts, trusting in God and the Laws of the great Universe. A seed of faith, once planted never dies. The tiny seed is programmed. It puts all its energies into bringing its inherent blueprint into materialization. It knows, trusts and acts. It produces without question, fear or delay. Affirmations, like seeds, often have a timetable of their own.

YOU GOT TO...

**Accentuate the Positive,
Eliminate the Negative.
Latch on to the Affirmative,
and don't mess with Mr. In-Between.**

Song Title: Ac-Cent-Tchu-Ate the Positive
1944
Music by: Harold Arlen
Lyrics by: Johnny Mercer

CHAPTER 6

Think About These

BIG LAWS
TO
CONSIDER

The Law of Cause and Effect

Another way of stating this law is simply, "What you sow is what you reap." What you do is the cause and what happens is the result of that cause, the effect. Sometimes, this law operates from a completely subconscious level – a forgotten fundamental part of your default programming. Sometimes you keep sowing the "same-old-same-old" and wonder why you always get the "same-old-same-old". It is simply because you are deploying the same unconscious programming. Affirmations can help interrupt this programming by creating a new program at this level.

The Law of Priming the Pump

In days prior to modern plumbing, if you lived on a farm, you had to do an action called, "Priming the Pump" in order to get any water from the well. First, you had to save some water in the pail from the last time you drew water from the well. Second, when you needed more water you had to pour the remaining water in the pail, down the pump, to prime it, so you could get the water you require. You were willing to do this knowing, based upon previous experience, you had to invest the water in the pail to get an abundance of more water from the well. Life is like that!

You need to invest time, energy, effort, to create the world you want, as long as it is to the good of all.

It takes faith and courage to step-out and invest in priming the pump of your future. There is always the oft chance that the well may have run dry and you have wasted the water. In such a case you may have to dig a deeper well or dig a completely new well. Regardless, you have to "Prime the Pump".

Pay it Forward
This law is closely related to the previous two laws. It is a conscious effort to sow good in the world to increase the reserve of good and generate more of the same. Think of paying it forward as planting a seed; a single grain of wheat, an apple seed, or grape seed has within it the potential to generate a thousand fold of its kind. However, this act of paying it forward may not be immediately apparent in its return. One pays it forward, not for personal gratification, but because it is the right thing to do. Let's say, when a person does an act of kindness, they feel really great after doing it and the other person simultaneously feels gratitude as well.

The Law of Association
You are judged by the company you keep. It is so important with whom you associate. Make sure that your friends and associates are supportive and uplifting. Remember you are identified by the company you keep. You are the sole decision maker and are accountable for your choices.

Law of Kind

In the natural world you will notice that similar species cluster together. In human relationships people of a similar mindset and/or behaviour pattern group together. Who are you hanging out with at the intersection of your life? This law is closely related to the Law of Association.

The Law of Attraction

Like attracts like.
More gathers more.
What you think about you bring about.
What you are seeking is seeking you.

The law of attraction that you are most familiar with from science is that "opposites attract". And "likes repel" The N. Pole attracts the S. Pole and two like poles repel one another. Human relationships sometimes follow this pattern.

At other times, you attract the person who is most like you, that is "like attracts like". This law is closely associated with the previous two laws.

Consider the old saying, "Birds of a feather flock together." The people that you most commonly associate with and are attracted to are people who share your common values and interests. You, as the sole decision maker, are accountable and responsible for your life's choices.

DISCOVER THE POWER OF THE QUESTION

Every GOOD STORY begins by answering these
KEY QUESTIONS:

Who?

What?

How?

Where?

When?

Why?

When you start writing your affirmation, consider
answering these SIX BASIC questions.

Additionally, consider the following

The Power of the Question

Question:

What is the one thing that I can do today to change the
experience of my life?

The Power of the Declarative Sentence

Declare what you are going to do and follow through.

The one thing that I can do today to change the
experience of my life is _____ ...and then go do it!

A KEY QUESTION

What is here for me to learn about myself, that is not
immediately known to me, in writing this affirmation?

CHAPTER 7

FAQ

FREQUENTLY ASKED QUESTIONS

Q.1 How many affirmations should I do at a time? Can I do more than one at the same time?

A. We recommend that you practice one affirmation at a time, especially if you are just beginning using affirmations. Doing one affirmation at a time will assist you in maintaining your focus and concentration, much like when using a magnifying glass to ignite a camp fire.

As you become more familiar with the affirmation process, you can work on more than one affirmation at a time, but be certain to deal with one affirmation individually at a time so that you do not lose your focus and create a state of internal confusion. Write one affirmation per page thus maintaining your focus and concentration on what you want to affirm with that affirmation.

Q.2 Should I start affirming small things first?

A. Yes, I would say that is a good idea. Also, at the beginning I suggest you keep what you are doing to yourself. When it manifests, then share it with everyone! The danger of telling everyone when you are starting your affirmation, is that, they may discourage you by a negative remark that could hinder your manifestation. By all means share your manifested affirmations with everyone.

Q.3 Can I do Long-Term Affirmations?

A. Yes, you certainly can. You may wish to do some long-term affirmations for projects or goals you wish to realize in six months, one year, five years or longer from now. Be prepared however, to change and update your affirmations as you change. Sometimes long term affirmations can and do manifest in the short term so be prepared.

Q.4 How long do I need to keep doing my affirmation?

A. Continue to do your affirmation until it manifests as affirmed (or better). When it manifests, rejoice and live in an attitude of gratitude. Remember to say, "Thank you! Thank You! Thank You!" to demonstrate your appreciation and continued readiness to receive.

You may have realized that the reason for the affirmation not manifesting is because you are affirming for something that you do not want at this particular time, or it is not to your highest good or life's purpose.

Finally, you may have simply outgrown the affirmation. Your interest or desire and focus may have changed. Your previous affirmation may have simply been a stepping-stone, a point of departure and clarification, to what you truly want.

FOLLOW THE STEPS OF THE AFFIRMATION CONTRACT PROCESS!

Q.5 Is there any correct way of writing and recording your affirmation?

A. No, apart from following the affirmation method outlined in this book, you can write or record your affirmation any way you like. You can use any type of paper, a scrapbook, if you're into scrapbooking; a sketch book, if you're an artist; or electronic (digital) means, if you're on-the-go. You can record your affirmation on your desktop, tablet, or smart phone. You can record it as your screensaver on any of these devices. You can even record, in your own voice, and replay it on these devices, throughout the day. You may even choose to email yourself your affirmation throughout the day. Remember to decorate and add excitement your affirmation by adding color, images, and/or your favorite music. These little additions will encourage you to regularly and faithfully repeat your affirmation, thus, completing the contract with yourself.

Q.6 Do I have to have faith to make affirmations work?

A. No, one is only encouraged to follow the method outlined in this book. Faith or confidence-building is something in which we all need to work. To increase your faith and confidence in this method you may choose to create a record book of all your affirmations that have successfully come to pass. To do this, get a loose-leaf binder and place all of your completed affirmations showing the date on which they were successfully completed. I use a big check mark with a felt pen to indicate its successful completion, or something better. Review this binder often. This builds confidence that affirmations can and do work for you.

This binder can be reviewed from time-to-time to re-enforce, in your conscious and sub-conscious mind, exactly why these affirmations were successful. The binder will help you identify the key characteristics of a successful affirmation for you. Also see **Q 9**.

YOU CAN WRITE A SUPPORTIVE AFFIRMATION WITH THE OTHER PERSON'S APPROVAL.

Q.7 Can I do affirmations for someone else?

A. I would say 'No' because we cannot do affirmations successfully to make another person do something *(perhaps even against their will)*, unless you have written the affirmation jointly and have agreed to say it daily. You could write a supportive affirmation that is in complete alignment with what your friend wishes to accomplish, such as an affirmation for health, career, relationship, etc...

This process of writing shared/support affirmations requires that you are both in regular contact with each other to ensure that the agreed upon affirmation is still being used.

Remember: The process of doing affirmations is very personal. It is always important to remember to affirm (order up) what YOU want--not what your parents, spouse, friends, or others want for you.

Q.8 Is doing an affirmation contrary to a person's religious belief.

A. No, doing affirmations is largely supported in many religious traditions. However, the acceptance of affirmations as an acceptable part of religious practice is often determined by the religious leadership in the various religious communities. It is best to consult your religious texts and leadership for guidance in this regard.

Modern psychology and psychiatry focus on uncovering a person's conscious and unconscious thought patterns and seeks to replace those negative and reactive thoughts with more positive and helpful patterns so as to improve the individual's life. It is, in short, the action of resetting one's default thought patterns to living a better life.

IT MAY BE TIME TO REVIEW YOUR AFFIRMATION. IS IT WHAT I NOW WANT OR SOMETHING BETTER?

Q.9 What do I do when my affirmations do not seem to be working?

A. First of all, review what you have written to make sure what you are asking is still what you want.

Be specific and say, "What you Want"!

Check to make sure your affirmation is created properly.

Look at the words you are using. Even one word can make a difference. Change the wording in your affirmation to more accurately reflect what you want to have in your life now.

Ask, "Am I rigidly attached to the outcome, as I think it should be, and all-the-while missing the completion of the affirmation or something better?"

As you get clearer about your affirmation and what it is that you want, keep on doing your affirmation. The answer may be just around the corner!

Q.10 Can I do a group affirmation?

A. Again, you can always do Support Affirmations and/or Group Affirmation where a group of people commit to affirming the same outcome and to the good of all (ie. Business or Community Projects, or simply supporting individuals in actualizing their affirmations).

See steps below for creating an Affirmation Master Mind Group.

Key Points to Creating an Affirmation Master Mind Group

1. Partner with members of like-mind who are committed to the best outcome for everyone in the group;

2. Commit to a precise length of time that the group will meet (weeks, months, a year plus);

3. Set clearly defined ground rules as to how the group will operate;

4. The format of the meeting (agenda or reporting back to the group, minutes to be kept, etc.);

5. Determine when you will meet (for breakfast, lunch, or evening meal). It is important that the group meet at the same time each week, unless circumstances arise that make it impossible to physically meet at this time. You could always elect to do a group conference call or skype/google chat meeting, so as not to interrupt the momentum of meeting;

6. Where you will meet (public place or in participant's homes).

Privacy and confidentiality must be a priority for the meeting to proceed in an open and honest manner.

Group members may sign a group confidentiality and privacy statement.

Breaking this agreement may result in the immediate termination from participating in the group's activities for the offending member.

CHAPTER 8

Distance Operator

A FRIENDLY REMINDER

Forgiveness

When you truly forgive, you release negative feelings, thoughts, anger, resentment and you clear the path for your affirmations to manifest as affirmed. *Not forgiving* is one of the biggest blockages to creating what you want. Consider this, when you forgive, you are the person who benefits the most!

The Time is NOW!

It is very important to affirm in the NOW. When you say *will have*, you are putting the manifestation off into the future. The only time we have is now!

To the GOOD of ALL

The phrase, "*To the good of all parties concerned* " is one of the most important phrases in the Affirmation Program. I refer to it as the *safety net*. When you say, "*to the good of all parties concerned,*" you eliminate the possibility of negative interference and blockages. More importantly, it assures that the affirmation is right for you.

Thankfulness

It is important to be thankful. Adopt and practice an attitude of gratitude. It is easy to give thanks after you have received the fulfilment of your affirmation. Give thanks three times after writing each and every Master Affirmation.

P.S. Consider This
Give thanks in all circumstances and be content as you await the completion of your affirmation as affirmed.

Daily Repetition

By repeating your affirmation the words sink deep into your subconscious mind where they take root, grow and become your new reality. Repetition of positive phrases increase the likelihood of the affirmation manifesting and eliminating (dis-empowering) any negative subconscious programming by setting up new neural pathways of thought and behaviour.

Please print off and fill in what you desire to have, be or do to make your life healthier, happier and more prosperous. Affirmations are very powerful so please be very specific when affirming!

SAMPLE MASTER AFFIRMATION CONTRACT

(Decorate and colour, as desired, to make your affirmation more attractive)

I, (your name deserve and now have/am

_____

_____

_____

_____

to the good of all parties concerned.
Thank you, Thank you, Thank you.

I fully accept

Signed: _____

Dated: _____
Witnesses (if desired)
Signed & Dated: _____

Signed & Dated: _____

When you sign and date this Master Affirmation, you have made a firm and binding contract with yourself, the witnesses and God/Creator, Universal Mind, Your Higher Self or in whomever you believe.

CHAPTER 9

Strategies For Living

POPULAR AFFIRMATION LIFE TOOLS

All of the Affirmation Life Tools VIDEOS can be viewed at
www.heretohelpsolutions.com

1. The 1% SOLUTION

One of my colleagues shared the following story with me. He said, "When I was lying in a hospital bed in excruciating pain, It was hard, if not; downright impossible for me to say, "I am 100% healthy." I just could not do it as the gap was too large. So I devised a plan as follows. I said, "TODAY, I am 1% better (or healthier) than I was yesterday." He repeated this statement with faith, passion, belief and expectancy many times during the day and it worked! Now he **is** abundantly healthy and still using the power of Affirmations. You see his mind COULD and DID believe the 1% as it was believable to him and immediately set out creating conditions in his body for his optimum health.

"TODAY, I am becoming healthier and healthier.
"TODAY, my thought-life is 1% more positive than it was yesterday."

When Carolyn learned about the 1% Solution, she exclaimed, "You mean I don't have to do everything all at once!" Until this point in time, she had always tried to do everything at one time and it completely overwhelmed and exhausted her.

2. CANCEL, CANCEL, CANCEL
AFFIRMATION
LIFE TOOL

When someone says something negative or hurtful to you, just say, "Cancel, Cancel, Cancel . . . that is not true!" Then immediately fill that empty space you have just created with something positive, such as, "I am becoming happier and peaceful." Always cancel and replace a negative thought with a positive thought.

3. SPIRITUAL DISINFECTANT SPRAY

Get a small plastic spray bottle Decide what words that you wish to tape onto the spray bottle; Fill it with water; Add some of your favourite essential oil.

When you think negative thoughts, feel sad, or disappointed or when someone says something negative to you, take out your spray bottle and spray the area, softly repeating the words, "I am spraying the negative comment or action and replacing it with a positive, uplifting statement." Never spray a person in the face!

Using the Affirmation Life Tool Improved Things at Work

Grace practiced this Affirmation Life Tool whenever she had negative or angry thoughts about her boss. In her mind, she simply thanked him for showing her respect and kindness.

He became so much nicer and respectful to her. She was totally shocked when she got a substantial raise even when no one else did. She felt better because she was *not* harbouring any negativity and as a result the quality of her life improved. She is very happy with this special life tool and uses it often.

Sandy Related the Following Story

"When my husband Greg comes home from work in a negative mood, when he goes to the washroom, I quickly grab my handy spiritual Disinfectant Spray Bottle and spray around his chair, saying, I am spraying your negative thoughts and feelings and I now fill the air with happy, positive and uplifting thoughts and feelings." She swears that when he returns to his chair in a few minutes, he is back to his normal, harmonious self. She tells everyone who will listen how well this tool works for her.

P.S.

She now has a small bottle of her SPIRITUAL DISINFECTANT TO GO that she carries in her purse to use when needed.

4. CLEAR, SEARCH, RETRIEVE AFFIRMATION LIFE TOOL

Use this Affirmation Life Tool when wanting to remember information that just seems to be on the tip of your tongue, but you just can't remember. Use this strategy for everything that you wish to recall or remember, to remember dates, names, things and information quickly and completely.

CLEAR - Clear your mind of worry and endless thoughts. Then say, **SEARCH -** Search for the answer in the filing cabinet of your mind. Then say**, RETRIEVE -** And when you locate the correct file say, "Retrieve," and then **DOWNLOAD** that file!

A reader reports, "I just love the Clear, Search and Retrieve Affirmation Life Tool and use it many times a day…It has been a life saver. I visualize the whole exercise in my mind making it very real, finding the cabinet, hearing the squeaking of pulling out the drawer, even smelling that musty smell when locating that file that has the answer to my question. WOW! How can such a simple exercise be so powerful and useful?"

5. CUP EMPTYING AFFIRMATION LIFE TOOL

Take one of your cups;
On masking tape with a felt-tip pen, write: *My anger, hurt and disappointment;*
Place the masking tape on the cup;

Fill the cup with water; Sit down with it in your hands and visualize all that excessive, needless negativity dripping into the cup. Feel all negativity leaving your body. Stay with it until you feel that you have released as much as you can for that session, then take the cup to the sink and dump the water down the drain, knowing that you can never get that water back and with it has gone your anger, hurt and disappointment. Then, fill yourself with positive, happy, healthy, healing energy in that empty space you have just created, trusting that all that negativity has left your body, never to return.

Cup Emptying Affirmation Life Tool - Improves Self-Esteem

Using the Emptying Cup Exercise, I poured out all the negative feelings that were sitting on top of my positive knowingness and success. Now, my feelings of self-worth, self-love and respect are surfacing. I am so delighted. I am doing better in every aspect of my life and I am so grateful for you and your writings and teachings.

Samuel, Student U.S.

Patrick, a retired teacher from Rhode Island shares his experience using the Cup Emptying Affirmation Life tool. "I always knew deep down inside that I was a good person, but it was hard for me to bring that positive feeling to the surface of my mind. I did this by doing the Cup Emptying Exercise that you teach. I spent hours beating myself up, why did I? I could have, should have, etc. Now that has all stopped! I am focusing on the wonderful things in my life and reaping the benefits. Please keep on teaching these truths. *Much affection!*"

June						
SUNDAY	MONDAY	TUESDAY	WEDNESDAY	THURSDAY	FRIDAY	SATURDAY
	1	2	3	4	5	6
7	8	9	10	11	12	13
14	15	16	17	18	19	20
21	22	23	24	25	26	27
28	29	30				

Note: We suggest that you repeat your affirmations at least once a day for a period of 21 days or more to form a new behaviour or habit and to break any harmful habit. Constant and consistent repetition empowers you a greater opportunity to create new and abiding habits and behaviours.

6. STOP SIGN AFFIRMATION LIFE TOOL
How I use the Stop Sign Affirmation Life Tool

I downloaded from the internet a coloured picture of a stop sign; pasted it on a piece of cardboard. I took a Popsicle stick and glued it on to make a handle. I put it by my chair and I made another one for my desk. Whenever a negative thought pops up, I pick up one of these stop signs, look at it and say "STOP!" Sometimes I visualize a flag person at a construction site standing holding a stop sign directing traffic.

If you are more kinesthetic (touch/feel), you may choose to do a physical action like snapping an elastic band on your wrist, clapping your hands, or stomping your foot to anchor the stop command in your subconscious mind to redirect your thinking. I have fun with this Affirmation Life Tool. Do it and see how it works for you.

Jack, a reader shared his story with me. He said. "One day I felt the beginning of a migraine headache." He remembered what I shared in a workshop about talking to our bodies and how powerful our minds are. So he said, with authority and faith, "STOP! There is no need for you to be here. You must leave now"- - and it did! He demonstrated the power of the subconscious mind which obeys the conscious mind when given a clear, strong instruction. How are you instructing your subconscious mind?

A woman who recently discovered the Stop Affirmation Life Tool, says, "I use the Stop Sign Affirmation Life Tool when I am focusing and/or obsessing on a particular negative person or event. I pick up my Stop sign and I say with authority, "STOP! All Clear - Change Direction, Thank you. *Ellenora*

Another reader says that she uses the stop sign process as a means to control physical pain. She says it is a very effective tool <u>as part</u> of her <u>pain</u> <u>management</u> <u>strategy</u>.

TWO FINAL AFFIRMATION STORIES

Joey, Known as the 'Class Bully'
After learning about our Affirm and Learn (Affirmation) Program that taught students how to be polite, get along with each other, and treat others with respect, he stood up in front of the class and said, "I used to fight a lot and I was called 'the class bully' Well, that was before I learned about those affirmations, the ripple effect and that we should be respectful and kind to each other."

A Note From The Librarian
The clerk at the Library, where the class visited once a week, called the teacher aside and asked her what she was doing with her particular class because they were so polite and considerate of one another. The teacher shared with her that she was convinced that it was because of the Affirmation Program that was being taught to her class!

<u>Consider This</u>

Practice using these Affirmation Life Tools and experience the positive results that others have.

notes

more notes

and more notes

and still more notes

Websites to Visit

www.heretohelpsolutions.com

www.annemarieevers.com

www.selfimprovementtalkradio.com

www.yourpassport tohappiness.com

Other Books to Read

To learn more about affirmations, read
Affirmations Your Passport to Happiness, 8th ed.

Facing a Health Challenge, read

70 Ways to Cope with Chemo and/or Other Medical
Treatments

email: affirmationbook@gmail.com

82175138R00039

Made in the USA
Columbia, SC
14 December 2017